INSIDE IBIZA

INSIDE IBIZA

EMMA ROIG ASKARI

PHOTOGRAPHY BY
RICARDO LABOUGLE

FOREWORD BY
DANIEL ROMUALDEZ

VENDOME

Contents

Foreword
DANIEL ROMUALDEZ 13

Introduction
EMMA ROIG ASKARI 14

RICARDO LABOUGLE 19

Party animals
22

Harnessing the light
36

Pursuing a dream
54

Brutalist opulence
66

Bringing the outside in
82

A house of wonder
98

Dusk till dawn
110

From the palace to the sea
126

A duchess's refuge
144

A reclaimed paradise
158

The jasmine effect
172

Bougainvillea explosion
186

A whim that became a passion
198

A treasure trove of memories
214

Planet Miranda
224

Water turns to gold
236

The victory of love
250

Carving shadows in the sun
262

Life steeped in color
274

Let the sunshine in
286

Seeking harmony
300

Settled since the Stone Age
312

Acknowledgments 326

Foreword

DANIEL ROMUALDEZ

> "Quietly elegant lives are being led in discreet corners of what has become known as a frenetic party island"

When I was lucky enough to visit the house of iconic fashion designer Jacqueline de Ribes, I saw Slim Aarons's 1978 photographs of her lounging on the terrace of her Ibiza home. Only then did I understand that Ibiza had long been keeping a secret—quietly elegant lives are being led in discreet corners of what has become known as a frenetic party island. For years, following the haute couture shows and fittings that marked the lead-up to the French summer break, the viscountess would retreat from Paris to the White Isle. It was here she chose to recharge, after a youth spent attending parties aboard Stavros Niarchos's schooner in the south of France or Carlos de Beistegui's balls at the Palazzo Labia in Venice. And when it was time for her to relax and retreat, she would nestle into her Vista Alegre hideout, tucked away on the remote south coast of an island with a notorious but mistaken reputation as merely a louche vacation spot.

Going to the surprisingly modest but clearly lived-in Ibiza home of the 18th Duchess of Alba, Cayetana Fitz-James Stuart, I tried to imagine her retreating there from the splendors of Madrid's Palacio de Liria or one of her five other palaces. While the house was more like a *casita*, its setting—in the most picturesque, serene cove, devoid of a single structure or beachgoer—was a dream.

The one house I wish I had seen was designer Jil Sander's Ibiza home. I can only wonder whether it was a minimal haven or a Mongiardino fantasy of an Iberian hideaway. It is exciting to imagine her spartan existence on an island where her fellow designers vacationed on the flashiest of yachts off its sandy coast—Valentino, Giorgio Armani, Miuccia Prada, Nicolas Ghesquière, all of whom I spotted on my daily pilgrimage to Formentera.

So I smile when my acquaintances in New York rib me for "slumming it" in Ibiza, thinking of it as the hedonism capital of the Mediterranean. Let them think that. Little do they know that here some of us fortunate souls have stumbled upon hidden corners of solitude, beauty, and repose unlike anywhere else.

12

—

13

Introduction

EMMA ROIG ASKARI

"This is an island steeped in myths, like the one that identifies the iconic rock Es Vedrà as the place where sirens sang to the hero Odysseus to sink his ship in Homer's *Odyssey*"

The Mediterranean island of Ibiza is a place of extremes, inviting many into its embrace while turning others off completely. Its power, appeal, and fascination are captured in the pages of this book, which invites you to look beyond the nightlife and flashy tourists to a magical world that lies in hidden corners of this beautiful land.

The Phoenicians settled here in the seventh century BCE, and considered the island to hold spiritual powers as there were no native plants or animals that could cause harm. They brought with them the goddess Tanit, linked with fertility, sexuality, the moon, and the afterlife, and worshiped her with debaucheries thousands of years before the arrival of Ibiza's nightclubs (in that sense, not much has changed!). Tanit is credited with giving the island a uniquely feminine energy, and her influence is still felt today, having survived waves of invasion by Romans and Vandals, Byzantines and Muslims, pirates and Catholic conquerors.

This is an island steeped in myths, like the one that identifies the iconic rock Es Vedrà as the place where sirens sang to the hero Odysseus to sink his ship in Homer's *Odyssey*. It is also claimed—though unproven—that Es Vedrà is the third most magnetic spot on earth, and that the legendary lost city of Atlantis lies underwater somewhere close by.

Ibiza was supposedly identified by Nostradamus as the last remaining sanctuary on earth at the end of the world, and it has indeed offered refuge for many in recent history, including Jews fleeing the Nazis, Italian artists escaping a fascist government, and young Americans evading the draft for the Vietnam War. When the Gestapo came to the island they were said to have been stonewalled by uncooperative locals, following in the footsteps of their ancestors who had similarly protected Jews from the Spanish Inquisition in the fifteenth century.

Ibiza has been leading the way for a while, with a culture of diversity and inclusivity cultivated over centuries that still defines the island today. It welcomed its first famous tourist, the Austrian archduke Ludwig Salvator, in 1867, and a century later the first gay club opened on the island in the 1960s, in the shadow of Francisco Franco's fascist dictatorship on the Spanish mainland. The local Civil Guard are said to have been caught by surprise, unsure of how to react to these charming, colorful new invaders.

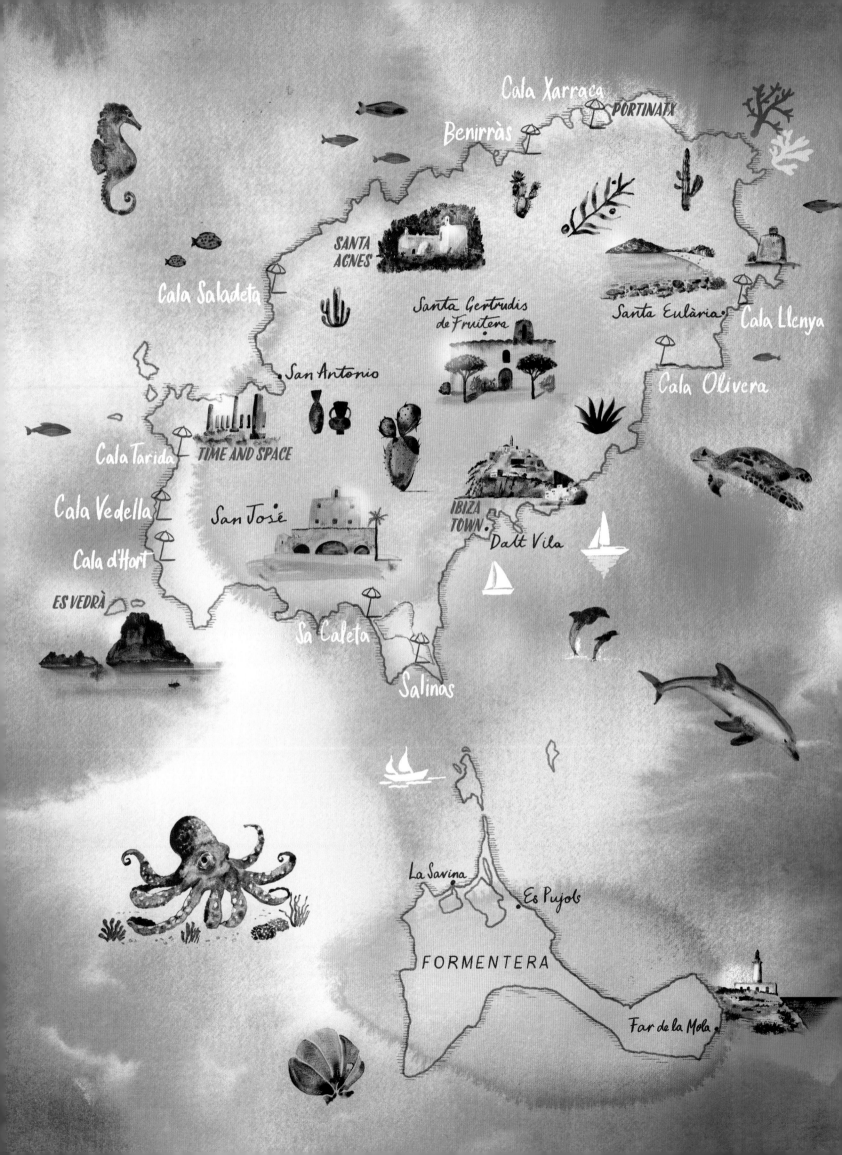

"The extraordinary houses showcased in this book were chosen because they represent the many kinds of diverse visionaries who have fallen in love with Ibiza"

It never ceases to amaze me that people focus on the party aspect of Ibiza, ignoring the thousands of years of rich history that came before the arrival of its "mega-clubs." The first of these was the legendary Ku, which opened at the end of the 1970s. James Brown and Freddie Mercury performed there and Grace Jones danced naked at one of its groundbreaking parties. The list of celebrities who experienced the magic of the island's nightlife at this time is staggering, among them Bob Marley, Led Zeppelin, George Michael, and Tina Turner.

But Ibiza's celebrity appeal had already been proven in the 1960s and 70s, with figures such as Romy Schneider, Niki Lauda, and Jacqueline de Ribes buying houses on the island, and Errol Flynn, Elizabeth Taylor, and Mick Jagger enjoying the pleasures it had to offer. Alongside the famous, the infamous landed here too, including the twentieth century's most prolific art forger, Elmyr de Hory, who moved to Ibiza to avoid being arrested. Orson Welles filmed his 1973 documentary about De Hory, *F for Fake*, on the island.

The extraordinary houses showcased in this book were chosen because they represent the many kinds of diverse visionaries who have fallen in love with Ibiza and decided to build their dream homes there. From a modern brutalist structure to an ancient finca with Stone Age bones buried in the garden, a Roman-era palazzo to a vision in pink, this island holds something for everybody.

Over the years the island has been given many names by the various cultures that made it their own—the Punics called it Ibosim, the Romans Ebusus, the Arabs Yebisah, and the locals Eivissa. This book aims to reveal its many different identities, to take you inside its many worlds. So, take another look at your previous ideas about Ibiza— I think you may be surprised.

RICARDO LABOUGLE

"As a photographer, it was a gift to capture each unique setting in which the homes are located, all bathed in Ibiza's magical and ever-changing light"

There are as many ways to see and experience Ibiza as there are people who visit it, but everyone agrees on one thing—nature could not have been more generous with this island's geography and its incredible landscapes. Despite having become a global tourist mecca, it still retains its unique identity and lifestyle, perhaps because few can resist the temptation to make it their own, even if just for a vacation.

Although the island becomes a bit more hectic during the summer months, tranquility and simplicity still prevail here in day-to-day life. Even today, locals coexist in harmony with visitors from every corner of the world, all sharing the same common interest in enjoying this slice of paradise in the Mediterranean.

Take a journey with us through these pages into some of the most spectacular homes we discovered across the island. Each of these homes reflects the individuality of its owners, who have freely reimagined the Ibizan aesthetic to align with their personal tastes. As a photographer, it was a gift to capture each unique setting in which the homes are located, all bathed in Ibiza's magical and ever-changing light. The houses encompass a wide variety of styles that reflect the cosmopolitan and sometimes eccentric character of the island, from grand palaces in Dalt Vila to more experimental projects, and of course those where Ibiza's hippie spirit of the 1970s can still be felt.

I invite you to explore with Emma and me some of the hidden corners of this island, and hope that these images will help you feel the radiant spirit of Ibiza.

Party animals

"A perfect playground for people to come together"

Bobby Dekeyser's Ibiza house is quite unusual—just like its owner. One day the Belgian-German entrepreneur was picking up his grandchildren from kindergarten on the island when he noticed two animals that looked a bit out of place with their surroundings. "There they were, two alpacas looking at us, and I thought, oh, that's a nice idea." Making the idea a reality, he sourced twenty-five alpacas from a breeder in Italy. They may not be the typical party animals associated with Ibiza but, says Bobby, "they really are the highlight of the place because everybody loves them—the family, the kids, visitors—and they provide beautiful wool."

Sitting outside on a massive bed designed for Dedon, the outdoor furniture company he founded, Bobby talks enthusiastically about his conception of Nay Palad Farm as an amusement park to entertain family and friends of all ages. Situated in the village of Santa Gertrudis, the charming house is furnished with objects from all over the world—especially noteworthy are the many pieces made by artisans in the Philippines, where Bobby owns a sustainable hotel. There is a tree house painted by an African artist; a yoga yurt; courts for padel, basketball, and volleyball; and an impressive outdoor gym. Unsurprisingly for the former goalkeeper of Bayern Munich, there is also a soccer field where Bobby holds tournaments with other ex-players.

Since buying the property as a traditional farm in 2018, Bobby has been extending and adding to the house and gardens constantly, with French designer Daniel Pouzet his most frequent collaborator. "It's never finished—I think it's boring when a house is finished. I get new ideas every day, like our natural pond for swimming in, surrounded by vegetation." Bobby's pet-friendly attitude also opened an unexpected new chapter for the farm. People began sending him animals that they did not have room for, which in turn started breeding. Besides the alpacas, his own Noah's Ark now includes two horses, six donkeys, nine goats, eight sheep, five dogs, and fifteen chickens.

Bobby loves having his four grandchildren roaming around his creation—"they are growing up in heaven"— as well as opening it up to his many connections on the island: "When we invite eighty or a hundred people to one of our parties there can be as many as fifty nations represented, with great musicians coming to play. This is a perfect playground for people to come together and share their ideas and experiences, and I love that." Is he happy? "As my grandfather used to say, I'm more than happy—I am content."

24
—
25

Harnessing the light

"I want a sunset"

"I want a sunset," I implored my husband, bringing him in 2013 to a barren, west-facing mountain on Ibiza. He was not persuaded. A small island, with a party reputation and only one golf course, it did not resonate. But the steep mountainside faced toward the coast of Jávea on the mainland, where I had spent my summers as a child and from where I used to sail to Ibiza in my teenage years. The island filled me with joyful memories and to have a house here felt so right and natural to me.

On untouched land we created from scratch a house with stunning views and—yes—a year-round sunset to die for. The house was designed by the talented architect Rolf Blakstad, in a process that could be kindly described as collaborative, as I was a client with lots of things to say. As Rolf has put it, "You were so much fun to work with, but tough."

For me, working with Rolf was pure bliss. As he was born in Ibiza, he had an incredible knowledge of the light, and in our first meeting he pointed out the exact arc where the sun would be setting through the year. "Yes, in the summer we were seeking shade and in the winter we were seeking light," he remembers. "The house is orientated to the west, so there were no issues during the day, but we had to open it up to the south for the winter sun. We moved the kitchen from the north side to the south as well, and you added the overhead light with the skylight over the stairs, inspired by the Pantheon in Rome.

It changed everything with the iconic staircase—that was your idea, Emma, taking inspiration from Valencian architect Rafael Guastavino's design at Carnegie Mellon University, built over a century ago. You'll remember we had to study his masonry technique. Well, that staircase has now traveled all over the world—I just built another one like it in a house in Arizona, inspired by yours."

That splendid staircase would not have happened without my sister, the designer Maida Roig, who directed the project. She found the proper artisans and constructors in our native Valencia, who knew the building techniques required to create the curves that date back to the time of the Arabs.

The interiors follow my obsession with whimsically collecting. For years I stored purchases made at flea markets, auction rooms, and architectural salvage sites in Paris, London, and Valencia. Anything beautiful that touched my heart would come with me.

The garden was a challenge. My friend the designer Hervé van der Straeten suggested we engage with the prominent landscaper Tania Compton. I was reluctant to bring a British expert to a Mediterranean garden until I learnt she had lived in Ibiza. Her knowledge of the local plants made the house complete.

After nearly ten years on the island, my husband finally understands its appeal—it is the unique pureness of its light, and we are so blessed in having been able to capture it.

Pursuing a dream

"There are still plenty of people here who were attracted to Ibiza for its nature and history"

Ève Cazes first came to Ibiza when her mother decided in the 1980s to buy a finca in the village of Santa Inés. After her mother's death, she sold the house in the countryside and fell in love with a nineteenth-century palace in the middle of Dalt Vila that was not for sale. Not ready to give up on her dream, she decided to rent an apartment opposite until 2016 when, after three years of waiting, the much anticipated "For Sale" sign went up and she jumped at the opportunity. She had finally bought the house that had captured her heart—only for the first floor to collapse, shortly followed by the second floor.

The house was originally built for a navy minister by Joan Gómez-Ripoli, who also designed other historic Ibiza landmarks, including the Teatro Pereyra and the legendary Hotel Montesol, both recently revamped. With the help of architects Victor Esposito and Pascal Cheikh Djavadi, it took another three years of restoration for Ève to make it what it is today.

Before deciding to settle on the island, Ève had an art gallery in Paris that specialized in vintage jewelry from iconic firms such as Van Cleef & Arpels and Cartier. She finds the freedom of Ibiza a refreshing contrast from her chic life in the French capital: "Ibiza doesn't like people who are stiff. However important you are in Paris or elsewhere, here you are a nobody. You won't be asked your name but you must have your own identity. People from all over the world move here because they are attracted to this attitude—it's all about being open-minded."

That said, things have changed since Ève first arrived. "I think there are now too many people who have a lot of money, and that has changed the island a bit. They want big houses and to be showy—it's all a bit bling. But there are still plenty of people here who were attracted to Ibiza for its nature and history. It's possible to live away from the nightlife scene. I think my husband and I have gone to a club just twice in the last twenty-seven years. And that is fine with us."

Brutalist opulence

"This island is filled with people who took refuge here because they were misunderstood elsewhere"

The renowned Mexican-German artist Stefan Brüggemann had no intention of buying a house in Ibiza, but on a serendipitous visit to the island he was struck by the magical possibilities offered by a plot of land. He immediately envisioned creating a garden with a house attached, rather than the other way round. Then the Covid-19 pandemic hit and Stefan and his partner, the photographer Fabiola Quiroz, were isolated in the land of their dreams.

"I liked the idea of the solitude this island gave us, which became a force for creativity," Stefan explains. The plot became his universe, and the soil his canvas. "I rearranged and reconstructed volumes of earth so you could see the flora at different levels and appreciate the range of colors." A circular pool of water is built like an amphitheater. The best view is when you are submerged in it, exploring the surrounding beauty. The pool is one of three circles. Another is filled with coal, representing fire, while the third represents earth. On that stands Stefan's aluminum sculptural piece *Trap Door*, which takes its name from the sidewalk entryways that drop into restaurant basements in cities like New York. This "trap door," however, is isolated in nature—a metaphor for the lonely descent into the subconscious.

The house, which also serves as Stefan's studio, was designed by Mexican brutalist architect Alberto Kalach and is made from humble blocks of cement. The living room is covered in gold leaf. Any movement of light is reflected on the walls, on which, at a close look, can be read Stefan's *45 Text Pieces*, with aphorisms including "Sometimes I think, sometimes I don't" and "To be political it has to look nice." For those who don't spot the engraving beneath the gold, the voice of Iggy Pop can be heard reciting them on a loop through speakers.

"People sometimes perceive me as a strange creature," says Stefan. "I can see it in their faces when they visit. It's like they are thinking 'I would never be able to live here,' but they can't deny its uniqueness. Walking around this home is like getting inside one of my works. Our place has its own language, its own DNA."

"This island is filled with people from all walks of life who took refuge here because they were misunderstood elsewhere, from intellectuals like Walter Benjamin to hippies and party animals, spiritual healers to millionaires. For its size, it is hard to find somewhere more cosmopolitan and varied. And when your house is the place where you want to be, you realize you are where you belong."

Bringing the outside in

"I wanted to do something honest and distinct, almost poetic"

"This house is all about a dialogue between the interior and the exterior," says Spanish architect and interior designer Amaro Sánchez de Moya of his clients' bijou home, situated in an idyllic Ibiza enclave. "It was important to me that all the different perspectives were connected in layers, guiding your view from the entrance patio to the vestibule, then the living room, the porch, the garden, and finally the sea."

The house his clients bought was neither old nor new, not a finca and yet not modern either, and it was difficult to grasp its identity. "Most people have an idea in their mind's eye of what an Ibizan house is, but they may be thinking of very different architectural styles," Amaro explains. "On the one hand, the local architecture can be simple white-cube structures, reminiscent of old Middle Eastern buildings, a look characteristic of farms in the countryside. But especially in the main towns like Dalt Vila, there's also an attempt at grand architecture, though sadly not much more than poorer versions of the aristocratic homes of Mallorca or Valencia. After all, before it developed a tourism industry, Ibiza was never a wealthy or sophisticated island."

Amaro was keen to avoid styling the house as a recreation of an imagined modern perception of Ibizan architecture. "I wanted to do something honest and distinct, almost poetic, while still incorporating the sophistication inherent in my clients' tastes and preferences." He created niches in the walls, a kind of cabinet of curiosities showing an eclectic collection that includes Renaissance ceramics, plates by Picasso, and a variety of African pieces, among other miscellaneous keepsakes.

He also wanted to strip the house of any references to historic periods or past styles, so there are no door frames, baseboards, or moldings. The doors are made with strips of oak stained to match the color of the sabina, a highly protected species of tree native to Ibiza. The gray travertine floors are cut across the grain "so you can't avoid seeing the parallel veins, which are so characteristic of the material. We chose it because it reminded us of the color of the stones on the nearby beach when they get wet." Live plants in the kitchen connect with the vegetation in the garden, and the unwritten rule throughout seems to be that the outside must be brought inside. In turn, the house reflects its harmony to the pines, the stones, and the surrounding sea.

A house of wonder

"We want to be guests of nature, rather than the other way round"

The story of this house began when an Italian couple decided to sell their home in Costa Rica and embark on a fresh adventure in a new paradise. "We reached out to our friend Pierre Traversier to see if he had any leads on properties for sale in Ibiza. We had one non-negotiable stipulation—the house had to be as close to the water as possible." That same day he sent them a picture of a house nestled on the northern coast of the island.

The couple—a property developer and a fashion director, with three grown-up children living across the world—immediately changed their plans: "Instead of flying from Costa Rica to London as originally planned, we changed course and went directly to Ibiza to see this enchanting place for ourselves." They have since made the island their hub. "The moment we arrived, our hearts were set. What we saw wasn't just a house—it was the realization of our dreams." Fittingly, they called it Casa Meraviglia, or House of Wonder.

They have deliberately kept the house as simple as possible, with very little color and using humble materials like a fishing net as decoration, in order to blend seamlessly into the natural surroundings: "We want to be guests of nature, rather than the other way round." Here the ever-present turquoise backdrop of the Mediterranean is framed by the distinctive wind-twisted pine trees that are characteristic of the luscious northern part of Ibiza. One of the family's favorite spots is the deck, where their daughter teaches yoga. It is positioned perfectly to capture the sunset, creating a space that feels intimate and yet infinite, where she can practice in complete solitude save for the sound of the sea and the gentle rustle of leaves.

"The peace and serenity that envelops this place is almost poetic—a stark contrast to the lively, vibrant energy of Ibiza in the summertime. It's like stepping into a different world, one in which time slows down and the chaos of life feels incredibly distant." Even in the peak of the high season, the north of Ibiza remains a peaceful refuge where nature reigns supreme. "The best part is that our home has a private entrance from the sea, ensuring that even when the island is bustling, we can retreat to our own secluded oasis. That is what makes this place such a wonder."

106
—
107

Dusk till dawn

"My days revolved around those glorious sunsets"

The first time acclaimed architect Daniel Romualdez vacationed in Ibiza in the mid-1990s, it was an unmitigated disaster: "My hotel room had a round bathtub in front of the bedroom window that could only be accessed by walking past a dark and moldy indoor pool." Luckily, a few years later his friend, landscaper Miranda Brooks, convinced him to give the island another try. She and another friend, Serena Cook, owner of concierge service Deliciously Sorted, introduced Daniel to a different Ibiza— "Suddenly I was in a parallel universe," he says. As a music lover, nights spent in iconic club Pacha were a dream, followed the next day with lunches of paella, accompanied by bottles of full-bodied Pintia and Pingus wines. But what finally hooked him were the sunsets: "My days revolved around those glorious sunsets, whose hour-long afterglow I would watch in my still-damp bathing suit—a sacred ritual that marked the end of each day and the start of each night."

There was no breaking the spell, and he went on a mission to find a place to rent. It proved to be a challenge: "I drove my real estate agent crazy, because I only wanted a house that faced those epic sunsets. Every year there was a different house, and every year I pleaded with her to find me something better." He committed instead to buy. "I wanted a two-bedroom house at the water's edge, with a view of the sunset and the legendary rock Es Vedrà. I was told that such a place didn't exist, especially in my price range. But I refused to give up hope."

Then one dreary January day his agent called—she'd found his house! On moving in a couple of weeks later, he found himself on a different kind of island. Instead of drought-scorched red earth and dust, the land was carpeted with acid-green pine trees and verdant fields dotted with white-blooming almond trees. He was in love.

A decade later, the house has changed his relationship with the island: "Instead of coming home from the club at dawn, I take early morning hikes on dew-covered trails. Instead of long lunches that take up the whole afternoon, I lie outside and read in the sunny stretches between light meals. Instead of dressing up for glamorous parties and fancy restaurants, it's pajamas and Netflix. The best of both worlds and everything in between can be found on this magical island. Where else could you say that?"

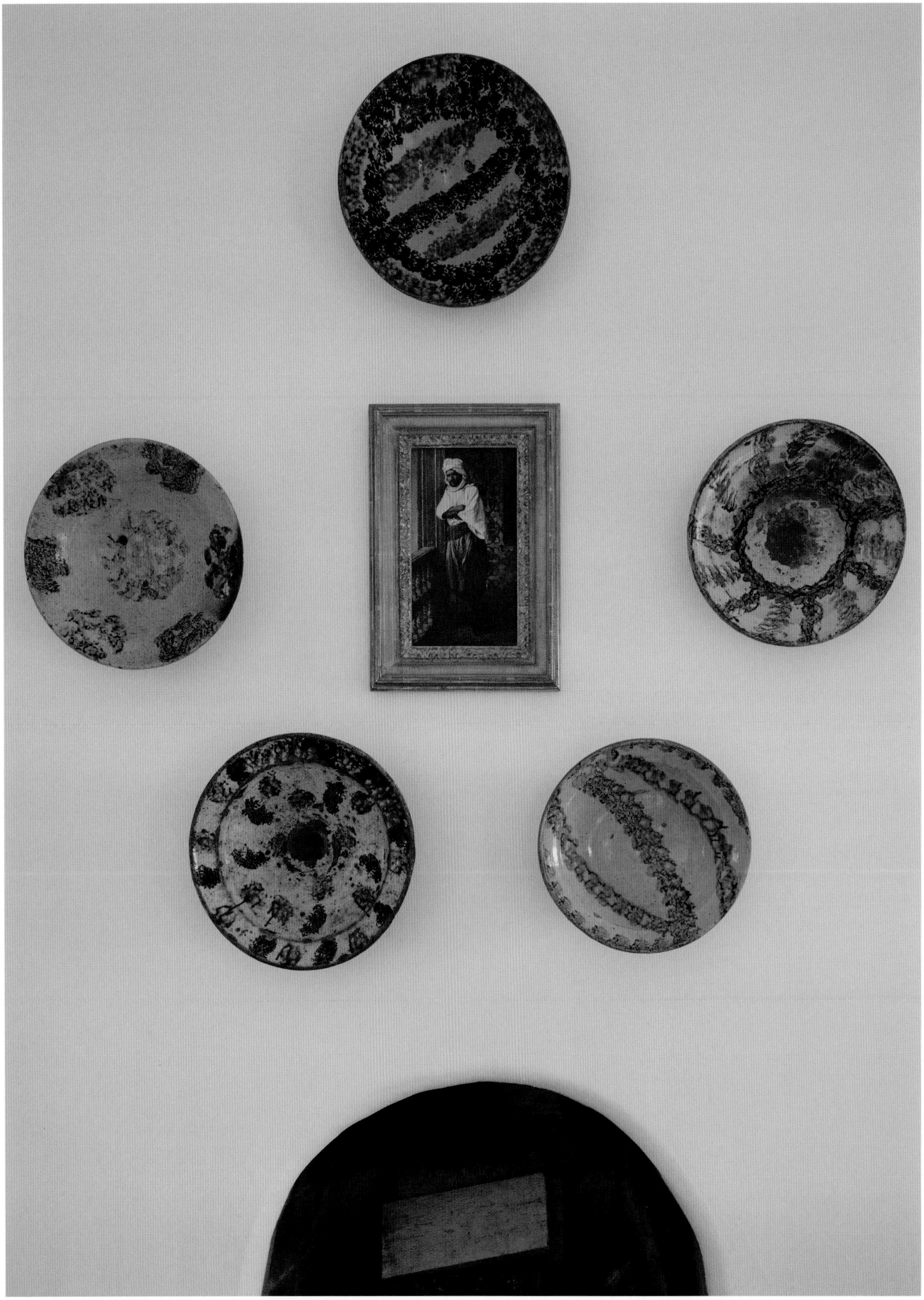

122
—
123

From the palace to the sea

"Everything had to tell a story—of the past and the future"

The designer Jacopo Etro is grateful that his father, Gimmo, found this derelict building when ascending to the cathedral on his first visit to Ibiza around thirty-five years ago. Overlooking the port, it fortuitously had a "For Sale" sign plastered to the door. With a vision of its potential, he bought it on a whim from the Spanish family who had owned it for generations.

The palace itself dates from the seventeenth century but was built on top of the ancient Roman walls that fortified Ibiza's Dalt Vila or Upper Town, now a UNESCO world heritage site. In making it their own, the Etro family was careful to respect and honor the site's 2,500-year history. While they naturally wanted to include the iconic fabrics of the family design firm that bears their name, they were clear that the house should never be a fashion statement: "The fabrics had to fit the mood of the house and its long heritage. Everything had to tell a story—of the past and the future—and yet feel comfortable at the same time," explains Jacopo.

They used colors traditionally found in the town houses of Dalt Vila, which are very different from those in Ibizan countryside homes. Terracottas, reds, and golds were favored, a vibrant and bold color scheme that nevertheless elicits a tender warmth. The palette beautifully sets off a collection of reliquaries: "We wanted some parts of the house to feel mystical, a bit medieval and ecclesiastical." Other period touches include the antique bargueño desk and the marble plaques and sculptures: "It's a bit old-school in a way, but being old-school makes it timeless and that was our aim."

Jacopo's favorite part of the house is the rooftop garden terrace, which is both lush and private. The family enjoys—indeed, insists on—having breakfast and dinner up there: "We're very lucky to have a palace in the old town with a beautiful garden overlooking the port. That is really the part of the house that we spend the most time in." It complements his other passion of sailing around the island: "There are lots of places you can reach by boat in Ibiza—Tagomago, Formentera, Es Vedrà. Beautiful, amazing beaches." And his home is just steps away from the sea, a privilege hard to beat.

A duchess's refuge

"To me this house captures her essence"

"This house was her refuge," Eugenia Martínez de Irujo, 12th Duchess of Montoro, reminisces about the Ibiza home she inherited from her mother. Eugenia's mother, Cayetana Fitz-James Stuart, 18th Duchess of Alba, may have been the most titled European aristocrat of her day—holding seven dukedoms, nineteen marquessates, and twenty-two countships—and yet she possessed a most bohemian heart: "My mother came to Ibiza for the first time with a couple of friends forty-five years ago and she was immediately captivated by the island. Very soon after she found this plot overlooking the sea and built this cute, low-key *payesa* house that reflected her soul."

In her palaces in Madrid and Seville the Duchess of Alba lived a hectic and glamorous social life, lavishly entertaining high-profile friends such as Jackie Onassis, Grace Kelly, Audrey Hepburn, and Elizabeth Taylor, and of course royalty, including the future King Charles III and his queen consort, Camilla. The freedom the island offered was the perfect antidote to her lifestyle elsewhere. Far removed from the demands of aristocracy, here she felt free to swim naked in her private cove and to fully express her unconventional flare without risk of judgment or compromise. Surrounded in her palaces on the mainland by Goyas, Titians, and Rembrandts, in Ibiza she could indulge her passion for painting, creating naïf artworks that still grace the finca's walls today, alongside others made by her daughter.

Since the duchess's death in 2014 the house has been maintained by her daughter Eugenia like a time capsule: "I've left it untouched because to me this house captures her essence. It holds so many memories. We started coming here when I was eleven. I remember spending every summer here, going to the hippie markets, walking around the old town with her. Getting to love the island through her eyes. Ibiza has changed a lot over the years, but not this place—this is where she was at her happiest."

A reclaimed paradise

"We felt a freedom we hadn't felt in other places"

Chilean Francesca Muñizaga and Spaniard Alonso Colmenares both arrived in Ibiza independently in the year 2000, and each fell in love with the island at first sight. "We felt a freedom we hadn't felt in other places," says Francesca. "What really makes this island special is the people who live here." When the couple got together romantically and decided to start a family, there was no doubt they wanted to be deeply rooted in the Ibizan countryside.

They found a farmhouse to the west of Sant Joan dating from 1870, in quite an unusual style for the island. But despite the challenges presented by the outside of the house, they couldn't resist the possibilities offered by the accompanying eight hectares of fertile land. Abandoned for forty years, they resolved to give the farm a second life with a permaculture operation. They planted 1,800 pomegranate trees, followed by olive and almond trees and an organic vegetable garden that now supplies many restaurants on the island with high-end produce. The couple moved into the newly restored farmhouse in 2015, a few months before their twins were born.

Alonso works as a publicist and Francesca is an artisan florist, highly sought after by large companies and private clients when holding events on the island. Francesca's flower studio is her pride and joy: "I think I was the first florist in Ibiza to grow my own flowers. When I was studying in England I had access to incredible flowers from a wide variety of local producers, but when I came to Ibiza I realized here they were all working with frozen flowers from Holland. The inspiration I find in my garden can be seen in my arrangements and connection with the flowers."

The couple keep the gardens and orchards as clean and simple as possible as there is so much going on decoratively inside the house. They don't follow any rules in their "maximalist" style beyond giving objects a second life: "We like old, used things—things with patina, with history. The decoration of the house is totally eclectic. There's no one style, it's just what we like, objects that mean something. Many things are from auctions or Ibiza's Sant Jordi market. We mix everything up in a way we think looks lovely and makes us feel good." Via reinvention and rebirth, Francesca and Alonso have managed to bring to life their own idea of a vintage paradise.

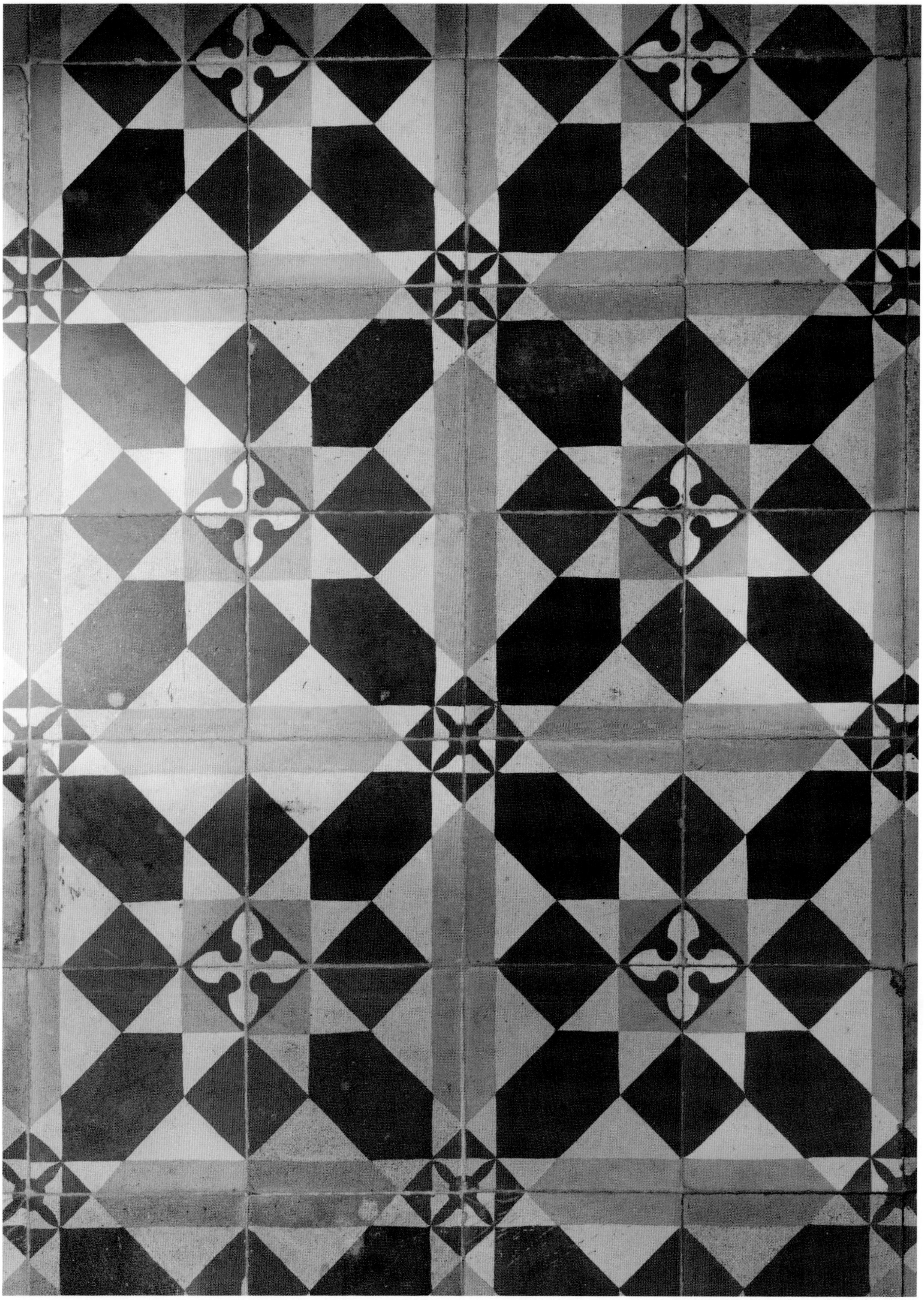

164
—
165

The jasmine effect

"I am lucky enough to live totally isolated in my Ibiza bubble from May to November"

"Walking through my home is like taking a journey," says artist Grillo Demo of his hideout in the north of Ibiza. He is describing the magical collages of objects and images that adorn the house, where Catholic saints compete for wall space with fashion icons like his friends Kate Moss, Elle Macpherson, and Naomi Campbell. Each corner offers a glimpse of the memories he has amassed through a life spent traveling. "If you were to remove everything inside, it would just be a simple cube in the middle of the countryside," he adds.

Argentinian-born Grillo has been a staple of the island since he arrived forty years ago: "I came to Ibiza at the end of the hippie era and at the beginning of the disco era, when everybody was chic and sophisticated." Since then, he has encountered pretty much every extraordinary person who has set foot on the island, but he holds a special memory of meeting the exquisite socialite and designer Viscountess Jacqueline de Ribes. Faced with the dilemma of what to bring to dinner for one of the most sophisticated women in the world at that time, Grillo reminisces: "I decided to make her a fresh jasmine necklace cut from my own garden. We arrived at her house dressed in hippie clothes, mixed with YSL and Montana, and waited for her to make a grand entrance down the staircase. And suddenly there she was, wearing a divine tunic. The moment I presented her with the flower necklace, she removed her jewelry and put it on.

I have never seen a more enthusiastic reaction to something so simple." The fragrant flower is included in most of his paintings.

Photographer Mario Testino has described a visit to Grillo's gardens as a must, rhapsodizing about how "the lemon, olive, and almond trees, roses, bougainvillea, honeysuckle, and every type of jasmine are a true joy for the senses." But such visits are now by invitation only. After decades of parties and celebrations, today Grillo prefers to enjoy the simple pleasures of painting his canvases and tending to his garden: "I don't leave my house anymore. I am lucky enough to live totally isolated in my Ibiza bubble from May to November, and then the rest of the year in Punta del Este." In both homes he has grown lush vines of the jasmine that will always remain his signature and lifelong essence.

Bougainvillea explosion

"It has given us some of the most incredible moments of our lives"

In 2007 the international couple who own this house—a financier and a fashion entrepreneur—were enjoying a quiet afternoon searching for a property in the English countryside: "We were reading *Country Life* magazine and an advertisement for an extraordinary property in Ibiza leapt out at us. It was a pure stroke of luck." The English countryside forgotten, they immediately flew to the island, realizing that Ibiza can offer an array of attractions more enticing than other Mediterranean enclaves.

Not wanting to be impetuous, they did their "due diligence," viewing ten different properties in just a few days and leaving the *Country Life* house till last. The fact that the luxurious complex in the southwest of the island was still being built was a major advantage for the couple, giving them the opportunity to customize and curate the home to their own taste and comfort. With just three children when they first moved in, they now have six.

The estate encompasses thirty hectares of beautifully landscaped grounds, with a tennis court, a nightclub, and a vast swimming pool that visually blends in with the seascape a short distance away. The house, which can accommodate around thirty-two people, has enabled the family to create a host of amazing memories: "It has given us some of the most incredible moments of our lives, with our closest family and beloved friends." They love to keep their home alive with parties—one of them attended by as many as six hundred people—and activities for all generations.

The couple appreciate the unique qualities of the island: "I think it is much more down to earth than places like Saint-Tropez or Mykonos, less structured and slightly more free-spirited. You don't have the kids in one place and the adults in another, there's a blend of generations and backgrounds. There are people here from all walks of life—artists, businessmen, some from the States, some from Europe or elsewhere. What they all have in common is the desire to enjoy life and the spirit of the island."

194

195

A whim that became a passion

"A peaceful retreat fostering a deep connection to nature and a simpler way of living"

The moment its Italian owners first set eyes on the finca Can Pep Pujols in 2014, it was love at first sight. "We had spent a few weeks scouting properties across the island without a clear idea of what we were looking for," remembers the husband, who grew up in Spain. "One realtor mentioned this old finca in Sant Joan, but she dissuaded us from seeing it at first as it was a ruin, uninhabited for more than a decade and overrun by nature. But we went to see it. The house was in a terrible state, off-grid, with no running water and the prospect of several years of significant work." Nevertheless, he and his wife made an offer within five minutes of first stepping foot inside.

Like all great love stories, the couple—a financier and a novelist and screenwriter—prepared themselves to endure the mammoth endeavor and the time and effort required without succumbing to its inevitable frustrations. The house spoke of centuries of agricultural labor, of making a living harvesting almonds and rearing sheep in a very rural area. Part of the building dates from 1743, but "although the work on the house was extensive, as a listed building it was relatively straightforward in terms of preserving and celebrating its heritage."

The grounds were a different matter, however, and required some significant reflection. With the help of local landscaper Juan Masedo, they planted a Mediterranean garden on a hillside replete with numerous dry stone walled terraces, each of which had to be patiently restored. Embracing the natural contours of the land, the garden is designed to enhance the stunning views at every level, with pathways winding through the terraces leading to secluded areas that blend the beauty of the garden with the wild scenery beyond. Native drought-resistant plants were selected to thrive in the sun-drenched climate, creating a lush yet sustainable landscape, each tier offering a unique opportunity to cultivate different indigenous species.

The love story continues: "Can Pep Pujols has become the heart of our family, a peaceful retreat fostering a deep connection to nature and a simpler way of living. It's where our children have learned to appreciate the rhythms of rural life and to understand the value of hard work and patience, and instilling in them a lifelong love and respect for the countryside." As Oscar Wilde observed, "The only difference between a caprice and a lifelong passion is that the caprice lasts a little longer." And this one is certainly heading that way.

208
—
209

A treasure trove of memories

"It is my bubble, and it really reflects who I am"

Argentinian-born architect and interior designer Luis Galliussi prefers to describe himself as a "curator of experiences." To enter his house in Ibiza is to embark on a journey across the world: "I am like a ragpicker who can't resist bringing back objects and furniture from all over the place, even when I have no clue where to put them. But at the end of the day, they always find a home." His Ibizan finca contains a whimsical collection of pieces from his years living in New York, Paris, and Egypt, where he sources his own finds, explaining, "I prefer to buy Egyptian and Moroccan pieces in their place of origin, rather than from Paris antiques markets." The house embraces these objects, which share its original and authentic character.

His decision to buy a place on the island twenty-five years ago was a spontaneous one. Over lunch, a real estate agent approached him at first with very flashy properties, having misread his taste and intentions. But finally understanding his bohemian spirit, she took him to some small ruins near S'Estanyol in the southeastern part of the island: "The old farmhouse was destroyed but the surroundings were unspoilt, with a valley that ran down to a small cove at the edge of the sea. I instantly fell in love."

This is how Can Kaki (named after his late canine companion) was born, and Luis has been making improvements and adding to it ever since, always preserving the essence of the house while incorporating a hidden layer of luxury: "At a casual glance everything looks very authentic, but my windows are fully insulated against both cold and heat and I have installed underfloor heating," he reveals. "All the work was manufactured to my specifications by local artisans from Ibiza and Mallorca." The result is a home that is cozy and pleasing to the eye but without any aspirations to perfection. "It is my bubble, and amid the mismatched curios it really reflects who I am."

Planet Miranda

"I have my own aesthetic sense and I don't like other people telling me how to look or behave"

Entering Miranda Makaroff's home is like landing on a different planet—the unique and inimitable Planet Miranda—with a kaleidoscopic explosion of color across every surface, even the toaster and the fridge, and pops of green and pink hues throughout. She came to Ibiza in 2020 with her partner, photographer and DJ Pascal Moscheni, to seek refuge during the Covid-19 pandemic: "Madrid was suffocating us, and we managed to escape just as Spain was about to lock down," explains Miranda, who looks like a modern, feminist version of a classic pin-up girl, a Betty Boop for the twenty-first century.

The couple found a very ordinary building high in the Ibiza hills, surrounded by vegetation and with an endless view reaching right to the sea: "We wanted to buy it so badly, but the owner was looking for an offer much higher than we could afford." That is when persuasive visionary Miranda came into her own: "I told Pascal, let's paint a picture of the house with arms extended as if it was embracing us. Visualize it—you, me, and the cats, with the sun shining in the sky." The magic worked. One by one the other potential buyers dropped out and the house was theirs.

Having grown up in Barcelona in a very creative household, her mother a fashion designer and her father a musician, Miranda reveals: "I was a bit lost because I have my own aesthetic sense and I don't like other people telling me how to look or behave." Rejecting an acting path, she began making daring Instagram videos, now followed by half a million people, which catapulted her as a young and independent creative talent into the world of influencing.

The house has witnessed, and perhaps even encouraged, Miranda's transformation from an influencer to an artist: "Making my Instagram videos is a full-time job that I sadly have less and less time for as these days I am much more focused on my tapestries and paintings." Now her art is praised by Marina Abramović and Madonna is on her speed dial. She recently painted a 115-foot-long mural for legendary Ibiza nightclub Pacha, and her work is shown in galleries in London and at Barcelona's Moco Museum, expressing her uniquely uncompromising, joyous, and colorful world. To put it mildly, Miranda rocks.

232
—
233

Water turns to gold

"Here we can serenely watch the moon rising in the east, before the sun sets in the west"

The hidden stone paths that wind across the landscape in and around Ibiza's Salinas salt flats hark back to a time before tourism, before the modern era even. For two thousand years the area has produced the valuable commodity, first commercialized on the island by the Phoenicians. Today, as then, the waters of the salt deposits reflect the sunset like a golden mirror.

With its double aspect, this house is uniquely positioned to offer stunning views of the landscape. The owner, a German financial trader who has spent his family holidays in the hills above Las Salinas ever since he was a teenager, still marvels at it: "The changing water levels in the salt flats and the changing position of the clouds and sun throughout the year create an incredible, unique spectacle every evening. On those long summer Balearic evenings when the rest of the island is gearing up for revelry, here we can serenely watch the moon rising in the east, before the sun sets in the west."

For him, this is the ideal location to spend his vacations, a place for relaxation, contemplation, and family gatherings. His favorite room is the kitchen, where his girlfriend prepares healthy meals overlooking the unbeatable views. A variety of lounging areas throughout the house and its extensive gardens invite guests to relax, read, and take long siestas.

But, he explains, "what makes this place so special to us is not the architecture but the memories. My mother bought this house in the 1990s, despite strenuous attempts by my stepfather to persuade her otherwise. She said she had a dream where an old woman appeared, imploring her to buy the house and commit herself to Ibiza. Without telling her husband, she went ahead and bought it. Sadly, my mother is no longer with us, but her irreplaceable presence continues to fill the house as we create our own magical memories."

He often rises early to walk the dog along the beach, watching the beautiful sunrise before the crowds descend. While the old woman from the dream never appeared again—her job was done—these glorious morning walks are just one of the legacies left by his mother, along with the resplendent golden sunsets and the joyful memories that will last a lifetime and beyond.

The victory of love

"In one summer on Ibiza the whole world passes through"

In Sanskrit, *shunya* means an unconscious bliss, a state of emptiness considered to be the ultimate goal of meditation. And that is what this British couple found—after ten years of searching—at Can Shunya, a finca located in the north of Ibiza, not far from the temple of the goddess Tanit. The house is one of just two on the island built with tachyon crystals, believed by some to promote balance and harmony in the body's energy fields.

As a foil to their very busy lives—he works as the global leader of a behavioral science and well-being business and she as a human rights lawyer—the couple love to escape together to Ibiza to recuperate and relax. They practice yoga and meditation daily, a treat for friends who come to stay, as they are welcome to join each morning before enjoying a roster of the best therapists on the island. "After years of trying other places in the Med we realized that, while there may be places that are more cultural, more beautiful, or more remote, there was nowhere that could compete with the unique energy and creativity of this island," she explains. "In one summer on Ibiza the whole world passes through, as its energy draws a stream of intellectuals, artists, and musicians."

The house was decorated with input from the Axel Vervoordt studio in Antwerp, Rolf Blakstad architecture, and fabrics chosen by the designer Sophie Hamilton. The couple have worked very hard to retain the essence of the property, with its stunning setting and Moorish history—hence the olive pots placed outside, the Tuareg and Beni Ourain rugs, and the collection of vintage Moroccan Tamegroute pottery.

Life in Ibiza has been even more enriching and stimulating than they anticipated, because the house's terraces are so fertile for produce. Accordingly, they have created a system of regenerative biodynamic farming, collecting and recycling rainwater and using solar panels to generate half the property's energy. Slowly they have transitioned almost entirely to dry planting, following the principles of Olivier Filippi's Mediterranean gardens: "We now harvest and bottle our own olive oil and citrus crops, as well as avocados, pomegranates, passion fruit, and three terraces of organic vegetables. The dozen chickens we keep are extremely well fed!" she adds, smiling. The romance they continue to share with their home is perfectly encapsulated in the Tracey Emin artwork they own that reads "Love always wins."

256
—
257

258
—
259

Carving shadows in the sun

"Our only requirement was for a home that reflects our lifestyle"

"It was a true test, because we are a married couple who work together as well, and in this instance we were also our own clients," says Spanish architect Jaime Romano, describing how he and his Ecuadorian wife, the interior designer Roberta Jurado, set out to build a house for themselves in the valleys of Pla de Corona, an agricultural region in the northeast of Ibiza.

They embarked on the project with the aim of creating simple architecture, with clean lines and large open spaces, like those they design for the majority of their clients, whose key concerns are the view and the light. But as they moved forward with it, their approach evolved, shifting the emphasis instead toward more privacy and energy efficiency, adding louvers painted canary yellow to block out the sun in summer and keep in warmth in winter. "We wanted to build a contemporary, easy house, not a farmhouse or a replica of an Ibizan finca," says Roberta. In doing so, Jaime took references from the legendary Catalan architect Josep Lluís Sert, designer of the Spanish Republic's pavilion at the 1937 Paris Exposition, a proponent of modernism who lived in Ibiza in the mid-1930s before being exiled to the United States.

The Romano house reflects its owners' personalities, with hammocks brought from Ecuador; ceramics from Andalusia, Latin America, and Asia; and a massive bookcase built to house Jaime's vast collection of books in many languages. Their sofa is made from recycled planks of wood, upholstered in traditional Mallorcan tela de lenguas, a fabric similar to ikat, which felt like a good fit.

Outside is a lush wild garden, with terraces covered in wisteria and bougainvilleas, giving off a fragrant, ever-present scent that lifts the senses and brings the powerful colors to life. Alongside, they planted 360 almond trees, as well as dozens, if not hundreds, of other indigenous plants, such as carob, olives, and fig trees.

The experience has changed them a little. As Jaime reveals: "I believe I am a better architect, with more patience, more empathy, and a greater ability to listen to the client, having undertaken the design of my own house, with no external limitations imposed. Our only requirement was for a home that reflects our lifestyle—controversial, eclectic, worldly, relaxed, and fun, while at the same time being structured, organized, and family oriented, all under one roof. That's us!"

266
—
267

Life steeped in color

"What people here have in common is that they have all been touched by the magic of this island"

Magazine editor and publisher Roze de Witte left her native Amsterdam when she fell in love with Pierre Traversier, a former basketball player from Martinique. Originally based in Paris, the couple found themselves longing instead for island life. The choice of Ibiza was a rational one for Roze: "It could have been Sardinia, Corsica, Sicily, or one of the Greek islands, but logistically Ibiza is much easier to reach." They looked at twenty-five properties until they found this ancient finca in a magical spot in the north of the island. If they had settled on Ibiza with their brains, they chose the house with their hearts: "Oh, it was romantic ... The garden, and all the flowers. The previous owners hadn't done anything to modernize it, and we fell in love with its authenticity," says Pierre.

Ibiza also came with other advantages for Roze: "I love having access to great international food— Lebanese, Italian, Japanese—and we enjoy the mix of creative people from all over the world." To avoid what she describes as "the crazy party people on the island," they went to the more isolated north. "I'm not attracted to that aspect of the island, so that's why we live on a hill, with nobody nearby. It's very close to the sea, and I love to swim every morning."

Having lived in the finca for fourteen years, another project emerged: "We had never thought about owning a hotel, but we saw this simple 1960s building with no character but in an amazing location by the sea in the village of Portinatx, and we couldn't resist rescuing it," says Roze. Giving it their magic touch, which floods everything in a rainbow of colors, Los Enamorados (The Lovers) is now a staple of the island, a charming hotel and restaurant along with a bazaar-like shop, skillfully curated and managed by Pierre, with stunning finds from Paris, Tulum, and Marrakesh. "I love the community here, charismatic people from all over the world, mingling together. What they have in common is that they have all been touched by the magic of this island." And that, he says, is just beautiful.

282

283

Let the sunshine in

"Every year we noticed we wanted to stay longer in Ibiza"

Looking to alleviate the winter months spent in Milan, the couple who built this house began looking for a summer retreat by the sea. "We were spending our vacations in Sardinia, Saint-Tropez, and Ibiza," the Spanish-born former model and mother of three tells me. "But every year we noticed we wanted to stay longer in Ibiza, so at some point we realized this was the place for us. The moment I land here, this island gives me good vibes."

Finally, in 2014 they found a heart-shaped plot of land that was blessed with the most breathtaking views they had ever seen. The next challenge was for her and her husband, an Italian financier, to choose an architect to take their vision further: "Patricia Urquiola was our first choice. Not only is she brilliant but, like me, she is a Spaniard living in Milan. More importantly she has been coming to Ibiza with her family since she was a small child. We thought she would be the perfect person to give us an updated version of a traditional Ibizan house."

While the stunning uninterrupted 360-degree views from the terraces needed no filter beyond the island's clean air, the light coming in from the outside had to be harnessed to divide the house into more private spaces. The result is an oasis that tames the strength of the intense summer sun, leaving poetic gaps. "Patricia's use of brise-soleils and louvers is so wonderful. The light entering the house is filtered throughout the day by all these windows, creating serene spaces with both brightness and shade." Since creating their home, the couple's love of Ibiza has not dimmed: "It is a special island where we are lucky enough to have a house that is the perfect base for us and our children." And rest assured that, for many years to come, the sunshine will continue to illuminate this magical place.

292
—
293

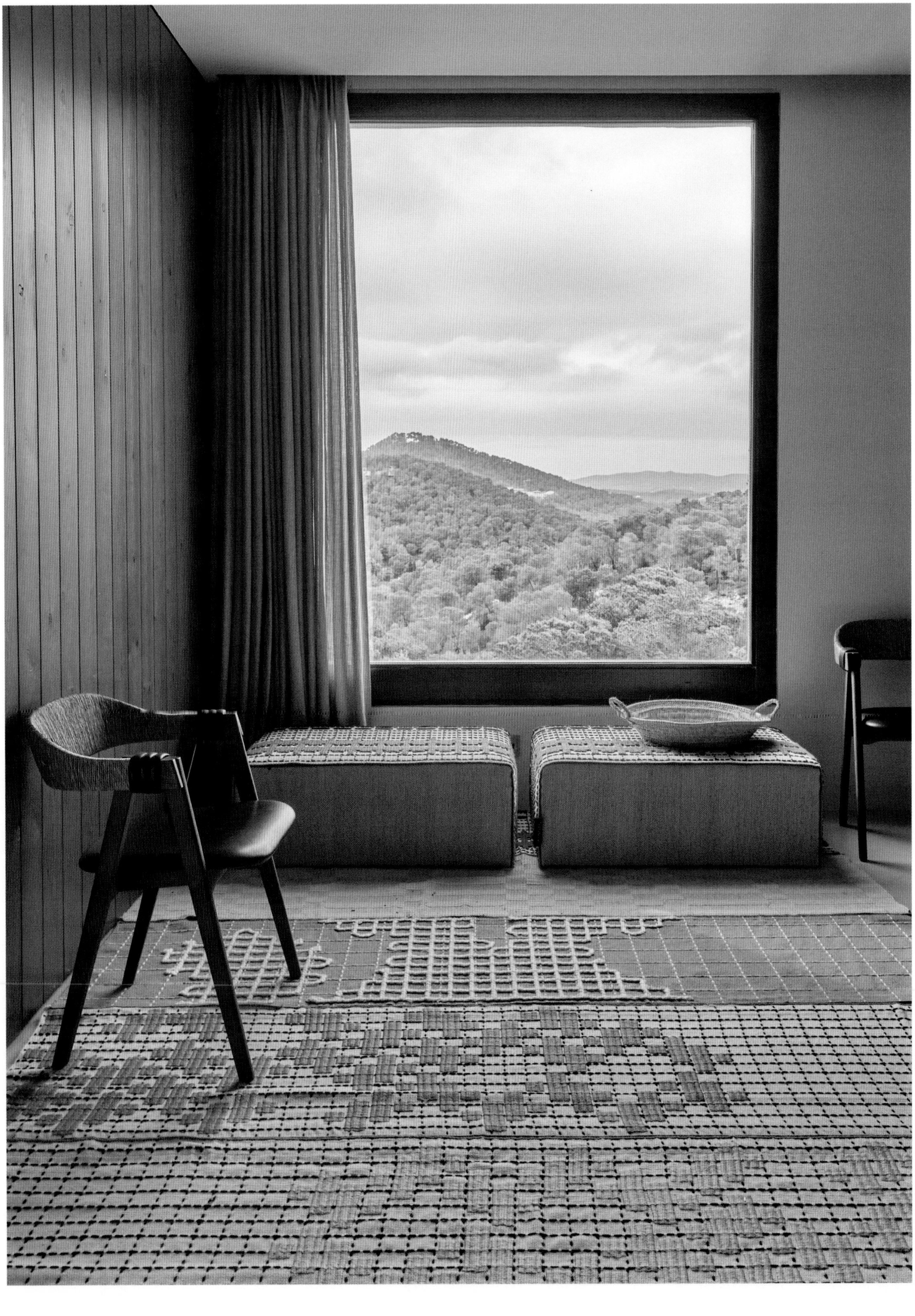

294

—

295

Seeking harmony

"The north is still very authentic—the nature is breathtaking"

French architect Victor Esposito revels in contrasts. Parts of Can Pep Beia, the finca he has lived in for the last twenty years, date from the seventeenth century, and the impressive arch over the entrance pays testament to its old-world architecture. But the historical style of dark, enclosed buildings suitable for agricultural life lived four centuries ago did not chime with Esposito's vision of modern living: "The rest of the building was in bad shape, and we decided to bring in light, opening up these massive windows that seem to talk to one another."

Esposito worked with French-Iranian architect Pascal Cheikh Djavadi to create the modern extension to the house that he shares with his partner, the German-born Moreno Castro. The idea to add a Japanese garden came after a trip to that country: "Not only do I believe in the spirituality it brings, but I also wasn't comfortable with the landscaper's original idea of planting an extensive fruit orchard, which would have required massive amounts of water, a resource the island is so short of."

Victor first experienced Ibiza when he was seventeen years old, arriving with some friends who had inherited a property there. "It was a life-changing experience," he reveals. He set his mind on living there one day and bought his first property at the age of just twenty-two. Life on the island in the 1980s was quite different from today: "There were open-air clubs like Pacha, Ku, Amnesia. You could dance while looking at the stars, and not one person was dressed in designer gear! It all felt very natural." It was Ibiza before the yachts and high-end nightclubs arrived, with their big-spending, distracted multimillionaires. But despite the craziness that now marks the Ibiza summer, Esposito still feels safe in the house he built and where he lives for eight months of the year: "When I am engrossed in the peace of my home, I'm not aware of how much the island has changed. The north is still very authentic—the nature is breathtaking. You just need to stay put with old friends who share your love for the essence of the island until the noise departs and the silence returns."

Settled since the Stone Age

"The fairies told her they wanted us to have this house!"

One would be hard-pressed to find a more extraordinary historic finca in Ibiza than this one. The house itself, Es Pouas, was built in 1640, but a cave on the site reveals evidence of human settlement dating back five thousand years, making this one of the oldest inhabited spots on the island. Victoria Durrer-Gasse, founder of La Galeria Elefante Ibiza, and her French husband, immunization pioneer François Gasse, moved to Ibiza from France in the 1990s. They lived all over the island—even on a boat—until they fell under the spell of this authentic property, untouched by what Victoria calls the "Miamification" of some Ibizan renovations.

"A lovely couple was renting it, but the day after we visited the man called us to say his girlfriend had been talking to the fairies, who told her they wanted us to have this house!" Victoria remembers, smiling. "He gave us the phone number of the owner. We did not have the money but took out a mortgage on our place in France and in 1997 we moved in with our baby in a sling."

Since then, the house has accumulated layer after layer of memories, represented by a treasure trove of objects collected by the couple on their adventures around the world, especially in Africa, where François spent much of his professional life. Alongside a collection of African tribal art, there are family heirlooms from India, where Victoria's grandmother lived, a table found at Portobello market, a Peter Jones sofa, figures of deities, a 1940s rocking chair, and a crocheted bedcover from Nepal. Victoria also collects kaleidoscopes, taking inspiration from them when creating her own works for her gallery. There are even pieces from the sea, discovered by the couple's son, photographer Emile Durrer-Gasse, on his freediving trips around the island's coast.

The world evoked by the cornucopia of objects in this house is one that the first settlers of this land five thousand years ago could never have dreamed of—proof that the attraction of Ibiza stands the test of time.

Acknowledgments

The experience of building my own house in Ibiza in 2016 and the love I've had for this island since I was a child were, for me, the seeds that flowered to become this book.

Finding our architect, Rolf Blakstad, was crucial to helping me appreciate the architectural history and aesthetics of Ibiza with its vast array of palettes and perceptions driven by the wide-ranging origins of the people who come to make this island their home. I am full of gratitude for my sister, the designer Maida Roig, who directed a team of specialist builders all brought over from my home town of Valencia.

A special word of thanks must go to my dear friend Beatrice Vincenzini, publisher at Vendome Press. It was her vision to produce a book on Ibiza, but one with some flair and whimsy. Thank you, Bea, for that vision and for believing that my passion for architecture and Ibiza would make me deliver a book on design notwithstanding my background in hard-news journalism.

This book is a collaboration and a work of love and grit by a special group of people. Cruising frantically across the island, operating under tight deadlines, was a joyous rollercoaster ride with the production team—the amazing photographer Ricardo Labougle, the optimist Gustavo Peruyera, and the ever calm and smiling Guido Vincenzini. No obstacle, including days of stormy weather, was too big for this dream team to overcome. No idea, however crazy or impossible at first glance, was too outlandish to try. *Mil gracias.*

My thanks to all the talented and beautiful people at Vendome Press: art director Peter Dawson; my editor, Felicity Maunder; our amazing publicist, Amy Tai; and production manager Amanda Mackie. I had never worked on a book before, so thank you for your guidance and your patience in teaching me.

This book (indeed, this island) is infused with the passions of the legendary Vicente Ganesha, the magical Serena Cook, the incomparable David Leppan, the wonderful Iker Monfort, the iconic Isabella Gnecchi, the knowledgeable Cat Cheshire, the charming Luca Romani, and the visionary Daniella Agnelli.

Ultimately, though, the true stars of this book are the owners of the many stunning and unusual homes portrayed across its pages. They all opened their houses and their Ibizan lives to us with generosity and love. I believe it is their devotion and passion for Ibiza that encouraged them to participate in this mad endeavor. My deepest gratitude to you all.

Finally, a heartfelt special mention to my family: my husband, Moon, and my three children, Alo, Clara, and Kito, to whom Ibiza became "home." Thank you for supporting my vision and commitment to this amazing island. I am so happy that it fills you all with as much love and joy as it does me. Let's keep singing at the top of our lungs our unique playlists when we drive around the island: Viva Ibiza!

Emma Roig Askari

Capturing the photographs for this book has been a joy. I would especially like to thank Beatrice Vincenzini and the whole Vendome team for their trust, along with Emma Roig Askari, Guido Vincenzini, and Gustavo Peruyera for their enormous help in the production of the shoots.

Ricardo Labougle

INSIDE IBIZA
First published in 2025 by The Vendome Press
Vendome is a registered trademark of The Vendome Press LLC

VENDOME PRESS US
PO Box 566
Palm Beach, FL 33480

VENDOME PRESS UK
Worlds End Studio
132–134 Lots Road
London, SW10 0RJ

www.vendomepress.com

ISBN 978-0-86565-439-6

Publishers: Beatrice Vincenzini, Mark Magowan, and Francesco Venturi
Editor: Felicity Maunder
Production Manager: Amanda Mackie
Endpapers and Map illustration (p. 16): Scott Jessop

Designer: Peter Dawson, www.gradedesign.com

Jacket photography by Ricardo Labougle
Front cover image, see Party animals (pp. 22–35)
Back cover image, see Settled since the Stone Age (pp.312–325)

Library of Congress Cataloging-in-Publication Data available upon request

Printed and bound in China

FIRST PRINTING

ISBN-13: 978-0-86565-439-6